50 Zodiac Kitchen Dishes

By: Kelly Johnson

Table of Contents

- Aries' Fiery Szechuan Pepper Chicken
- Taurus' Truffle Butter Steak
- Gemini's Dual-Flavored Sushi Rolls
- Cancer's Comforting Lobster Bisque
- Leo's Bold Honey-Glazed BBQ Ribs
- Virgo's Elegant Herb-Crusted Salmon
- Libra's Balanced Sweet and Savory Tart
- Scorpio's Intense Blackened Cajun Shrimp
- Sagittarius' Adventurous Moroccan Tagine
- Capricorn's Classic Beef Wellington
- Aquarius' Innovative Vegan Jackfruit Tacos
- Pisces' Dreamy Coconut Shrimp Curry
- Aries' Spicy Chorizo and Egg Breakfast Burrito
- Taurus' Rich Dark Chocolate Mousse
- Gemini's Yin-Yang Black & White Pasta
- Cancer's Homey Baked Mac and Cheese
- Leo's Show-Stopping Flambéed Bananas Foster
- Virgo's Fresh Zucchini and Pesto Pasta
- Libra's Harmonious Fig and Prosciutto Flatbread
- Scorpio's Mysterious Charcoal-Grilled Ribeye
- Sagittarius' Wanderlust-Inspired Paella
- Capricorn's Refined Mushroom Risotto
- Aquarius' Out-of-the-Box Lavender Lemonade
- Pisces' Mystical Seaweed and Miso Soup
- Aries' Red Hot Buffalo Wings
- Taurus' Decadent Triple-Cheese Fondue
- Gemini's Playful Mixed Berry Parfait
- Cancer's Nostalgic Apple Pie
- Leo's Bold Espresso-Rubbed Brisket
- Virgo's Artisanal Avocado Toast
- Libra's Graceful Raspberry Rose Pavlova
- Scorpio's Dark Chocolate Chili Cake
- Sagittarius' Exotic Thai Green Curry
- Capricorn's Sophisticated Truffle Gnocchi
- Aquarius' Inventive Miso Caramel Ice Cream

- Pisces' Ethereal Blue Butterfly Pea Tea
- Aries' Spicy Kimchi Fried Rice
- Taurus' Luxurious Lobster Thermidor
- Gemini's Contrasting Sweet & Spicy Tofu Stir-Fry
- Cancer's Cozy Clam Chowder in a Bread Bowl
- Leo's Majestic Gold-Dusted Crème Brûlée
- Virgo's Wholesome Grain Buddha Bowl
- Libra's Aesthetically Pleasing Charcuterie Board
- Scorpio's Seductive Dark Cherry Reduction Steak
- Sagittarius' Global Street Food Sampler
- Capricorn's Well-Crafted Classic French Onion Soup
- Aquarius' Unique Purple Sweet Potato Gnocchi
- Pisces' Ocean-Inspired Blueberry Glazed Salmon
- Aries' Bold Sriracha-Lime Chicken Skewers
- Taurus' Indulgent Slow-Cooked Short Ribs

Aries' Fiery Szechuan Pepper Chicken

Ingredients:

- 2 chicken breasts, cubed
- 1 tbsp Szechuan peppercorns, toasted and crushed
- 2 tbsp soy sauce
- 1 tbsp rice vinegar
- 1 tbsp chili oil
- 3 cloves garlic, minced
- 1-inch ginger, minced
- 1 tbsp cornstarch
- 1 tbsp vegetable oil
- 1 tsp honey

Instructions:

1. Toss chicken in cornstarch.
2. Heat oil in a pan, stir-fry garlic, ginger, and Szechuan peppercorns.
3. Add chicken and cook until golden.
4. Pour in soy sauce, vinegar, chili oil, and honey. Stir-fry until coated.

Taurus' Truffle Butter Steak

Ingredients:

- 2 ribeye steaks
- 2 tbsp butter
- 1 tbsp truffle oil
- 1 tsp sea salt
- ½ tsp black pepper
- 1 sprig rosemary

Instructions:

1. Season steak with salt and pepper.
2. Sear in a hot skillet for 3-4 minutes per side.
3. Melt butter with truffle oil and rosemary, then drizzle over steak.

Gemini's Dual-Flavored Sushi Rolls

Ingredients:

- 1 cup sushi rice, cooked
- 2 nori sheets
- ½ avocado, sliced
- ½ cucumber, julienned
- 4 shrimp tempura
- 4 slices smoked salmon
- 1 tbsp spicy mayo
- 1 tbsp eel sauce

Instructions:

1. Spread rice over nori.
2. Fill one roll with shrimp tempura and spicy mayo, the other with smoked salmon and eel sauce.
3. Roll tightly, slice, and serve.

Cancer's Comforting Lobster Bisque

Ingredients:

- 1 lobster tail
- 2 tbsp butter
- 1 shallot, minced
- 1 garlic clove, minced
- 1 cup seafood stock
- ½ cup heavy cream
- ¼ cup white wine
- 1 tsp tomato paste
- ½ tsp paprika

Instructions:

1. Sauté shallots, garlic, and tomato paste in butter.
2. Add wine, stock, and lobster. Simmer for 10 minutes.
3. Remove lobster, blend the soup, and stir in cream.
4. Add chopped lobster back and serve.

Leo's Bold Honey-Glazed BBQ Ribs

Ingredients:

- 2 lbs baby back ribs
- ½ cup honey
- ¼ cup soy sauce
- ¼ cup ketchup
- 1 tbsp Dijon mustard
- 1 tbsp smoked paprika
- 1 tsp black pepper

Instructions:

1. Mix honey, soy sauce, ketchup, mustard, and spices.
2. Coat ribs and marinate for 2 hours.
3. Grill or bake at 300°F (150°C) for 2.5 hours, basting frequently.

Virgo's Elegant Herb-Crusted Salmon

Ingredients:

- 2 salmon fillets
- 2 tbsp breadcrumbs
- 1 tbsp fresh parsley, chopped
- 1 tbsp fresh dill, chopped
- 1 tbsp olive oil
- 1 tsp lemon zest
- ½ tsp salt

Instructions:

1. Mix breadcrumbs, herbs, lemon zest, and olive oil.
2. Press mixture onto salmon.
3. Bake at 375°F (190°C) for 12-15 minutes.

Libra's Balanced Sweet and Savory Tart

Ingredients:

- 1 sheet puff pastry
- ½ cup goat cheese
- ½ cup caramelized onions
- ½ cup sliced figs
- 1 tbsp honey

Instructions:

1. Roll out puff pastry and bake for 10 minutes at 375°F (190°C).
2. Spread goat cheese, add onions and figs, and drizzle with honey.
3. Bake for another 10 minutes.

Scorpio's Intense Blackened Cajun Shrimp

Ingredients:

- 12 large shrimp
- 1 tbsp Cajun seasoning
- 1 tsp smoked paprika
- 1 tbsp olive oil
- ½ tsp cayenne pepper

Instructions:

1. Coat shrimp in Cajun seasoning, paprika, and cayenne.
2. Sear in a hot pan for 2-3 minutes per side.

Sagittarius' Adventurous Moroccan Tagine

Ingredients:

- 1 lb lamb, cubed
- 1 onion, diced
- 2 cloves garlic, minced
- 1 tsp cinnamon
- 1 tsp cumin
- ½ tsp turmeric
- 1 cup chickpeas
- ½ cup dried apricots
- 1 cup vegetable broth

Instructions:

1. Brown lamb, then sauté onions and garlic.
2. Add spices, chickpeas, apricots, and broth.
3. Simmer for 1 hour until tender.

Capricorn's Classic Beef Wellington

Ingredients:

- 2 beef tenderloin steaks
- 2 tbsp Dijon mustard
- ½ cup mushrooms, finely chopped
- 1 puff pastry sheet
- 1 egg, beaten

Instructions:

1. Sear steaks and coat with mustard.
2. Sauté mushrooms until dry, then spread over pastry.
3. Wrap steaks in pastry, brush with egg wash, and bake at 400°F (200°C) for 25 minutes.

Aquarius' Innovative Vegan Jackfruit Tacos

Ingredients:

- 2 cups canned jackfruit, drained and shredded
- 1 tbsp olive oil
- 1 tsp smoked paprika
- 1 tsp cumin
- ½ tsp chili powder
- ½ cup salsa
- 6 small corn tortillas
- ½ cup shredded cabbage
- ¼ cup diced avocado

Instructions:

1. Sauté jackfruit in oil with paprika, cumin, and chili powder.
2. Add salsa and simmer for 10 minutes.
3. Assemble tacos with jackfruit, cabbage, and avocado.

Pisces' Dreamy Coconut Shrimp Curry

Ingredients:

- 1 lb shrimp, peeled and deveined
- 1 tbsp coconut oil
- 1 small onion, diced
- 2 cloves garlic, minced
- 1 tbsp red curry paste
- 1 can coconut milk
- 1 tbsp fish sauce
- ½ tsp turmeric
- 1 cup bell peppers, sliced

Instructions:

1. Sauté onion and garlic in coconut oil.
2. Add curry paste, coconut milk, fish sauce, turmeric, and bell peppers.
3. Simmer shrimp for 5 minutes until cooked through.

Aries' Spicy Chorizo and Egg Breakfast Burrito

Ingredients:

- 4 large eggs
- ½ cup cooked chorizo
- ¼ cup diced onions
- ¼ cup shredded cheese
- 4 flour tortillas
- 1 tbsp hot sauce

Instructions:

1. Scramble eggs with chorizo and onions.
2. Fill tortillas with egg mixture, cheese, and hot sauce.
3. Roll up and serve warm.

Taurus' Rich Dark Chocolate Mousse

Ingredients:

- 4 oz dark chocolate, melted
- 1 cup heavy cream
- 2 tbsp sugar
- 1 tsp vanilla extract

Instructions:

1. Whip heavy cream with sugar and vanilla.
2. Fold in melted chocolate until smooth.
3. Chill for 1 hour before serving.

Gemini's Yin-Yang Black & White Pasta

Ingredients:

- 4 oz squid ink pasta
- 4 oz regular fettuccine
- 2 tbsp olive oil
- 2 cloves garlic, minced
- ½ cup cherry tomatoes, halved
- ¼ cup Parmesan cheese

Instructions:

1. Cook both pastas separately, then combine.
2. Sauté garlic in olive oil, add tomatoes.
3. Toss with pasta and sprinkle with Parmesan.

Cancer's Homey Baked Mac and Cheese

Ingredients:

- 2 cups elbow macaroni
- 2 cups shredded cheddar
- 1 cup milk
- 2 tbsp butter
- 1 tsp mustard powder
- ½ cup breadcrumbs

Instructions:

1. Cook pasta, drain, and mix with cheese, milk, butter, and mustard powder.
2. Pour into a baking dish, top with breadcrumbs.
3. Bake at 375°F (190°C) for 20 minutes.

Leo's Show-Stopping Flambéed Bananas Foster

Ingredients:

- 2 bananas, sliced
- 2 tbsp butter
- ¼ cup brown sugar
- ¼ cup dark rum
- ½ tsp cinnamon
- Vanilla ice cream

Instructions:

1. Melt butter, add brown sugar and bananas.
2. Pour in rum and carefully ignite.
3. Serve over vanilla ice cream.

Virgo's Fresh Zucchini and Pesto Pasta

Ingredients:

- 8 oz spaghetti
- 1 zucchini, spiralized
- ¼ cup basil pesto
- ¼ cup grated Parmesan

Instructions:

1. Cook spaghetti, drain, and mix with zucchini.
2. Stir in pesto and top with Parmesan.

Libra's Harmonious Fig and Prosciutto Flatbread

Ingredients:

- 1 flatbread
- ½ cup goat cheese
- ¼ cup sliced figs
- 2 slices prosciutto
- 1 tbsp honey

Instructions:

1. Spread goat cheese over flatbread.
2. Add figs and prosciutto.
3. Drizzle with honey and bake at 375°F (190°C) for 10 minutes.

Scorpio's Mysterious Charcoal-Grilled Ribeye

Ingredients:

- 2 ribeye steaks
- 1 tbsp charcoal-infused salt
- 1 tsp black pepper
- 1 tbsp olive oil

Instructions:

1. Season steaks with salt and pepper.
2. Grill over high heat for 3-4 minutes per side.

Sagittarius' Wanderlust-Inspired Paella

Ingredients:

- 1 cup Arborio rice
- 2 cups seafood broth
- ½ lb shrimp
- ½ lb mussels
- 1 red bell pepper, sliced
- 1 tsp saffron
- ½ cup peas

Instructions:

1. Sauté rice with saffron and bell peppers.
2. Add broth and simmer for 15 minutes.
3. Add seafood and peas, cook until done.

Capricorn's Refined Mushroom Risotto

Ingredients:

- 1 cup Arborio rice
- 2 tbsp butter
- 1 small onion, diced
- 2 cloves garlic, minced
- 1 cup mixed mushrooms, sliced
- ½ cup white wine
- 3 cups vegetable broth
- ½ cup Parmesan cheese
- Salt and pepper to taste

Instructions:

1. Sauté onions, garlic, and mushrooms in butter.
2. Add rice and cook for 2 minutes, then deglaze with wine.
3. Slowly add broth, stirring until absorbed.
4. Stir in Parmesan, season, and serve.

Aquarius' Out-of-the-Box Lavender Lemonade

Ingredients:

- 4 cups water
- ½ cup fresh lemon juice
- ¼ cup honey or sugar
- 1 tbsp dried lavender
- Ice cubes

Instructions:

1. Boil 1 cup of water with lavender, let steep, then strain.
2. Mix with lemon juice, honey, and remaining water.
3. Serve over ice.

Pisces' Mystical Seaweed and Miso Soup

Ingredients:

- 4 cups dashi or vegetable broth
- 2 tbsp white miso paste
- ½ cup dried seaweed, rehydrated
- ½ cup cubed tofu
- 2 green onions, sliced

Instructions:

1. Heat broth and dissolve miso paste.
2. Add seaweed, tofu, and green onions.
3. Simmer for 5 minutes, then serve.

Aries' Red Hot Buffalo Wings

Ingredients:

- 1 lb chicken wings
- ½ cup hot sauce
- 2 tbsp butter, melted
- 1 tsp garlic powder
- ½ tsp cayenne pepper

Instructions:

1. Bake wings at 400°F (200°C) for 30 minutes.
2. Toss in melted butter, hot sauce, garlic powder, and cayenne.
3. Bake for another 10 minutes, then serve.

Taurus' Decadent Triple-Cheese Fondue

Ingredients:

- 1 cup Gruyère cheese, shredded
- 1 cup cheddar cheese, shredded
- 1 cup mozzarella, shredded
- 1 cup white wine
- 1 tbsp cornstarch

Instructions:

1. Heat wine in a pot, then gradually stir in cheese.
2. Mix cornstarch with a little water and stir in.
3. Serve with bread and vegetables for dipping.

Gemini's Playful Mixed Berry Parfait

Ingredients:

- 1 cup Greek yogurt
- ½ cup mixed berries (strawberries, blueberries, raspberries)
- ¼ cup granola
- 1 tbsp honey

Instructions:

1. Layer yogurt, berries, and granola in a glass.
2. Drizzle with honey and serve.

Cancer's Nostalgic Apple Pie

Ingredients:

- 1 pie crust
- 4 apples, sliced
- ½ cup sugar
- 1 tsp cinnamon
- 1 tbsp flour
- 1 tbsp butter, melted

Instructions:

1. Toss apples with sugar, cinnamon, and flour.
2. Fill pie crust, brush with melted butter, and bake at 375°F (190°C) for 40 minutes.

Leo's Bold Espresso-Rubbed Brisket

Ingredients:

- 2 lbs brisket
- 2 tbsp espresso powder
- 1 tbsp smoked paprika
- 1 tbsp brown sugar
- 1 tsp salt
- 1 tsp black pepper

Instructions:

1. Rub brisket with all ingredients and let sit for 1 hour.
2. Roast at 300°F (150°C) for 3-4 hours until tender.

Virgo's Artisanal Avocado Toast

Ingredients:

- 2 slices sourdough bread
- 1 ripe avocado
- ½ tsp lemon juice
- ¼ tsp chili flakes
- 1 tbsp feta cheese

Instructions:

1. Toast bread, mash avocado with lemon juice.
2. Spread on toast, top with chili flakes and feta.

Libra's Graceful Raspberry Rose Pavlova

Ingredients:

- 3 egg whites
- ¾ cup sugar
- 1 tsp white vinegar
- ½ tsp rose water
- 1 cup whipped cream
- ½ cup raspberries

Instructions:

1. Whisk egg whites and sugar to stiff peaks.
2. Fold in vinegar and rose water, shape into a nest.
3. Bake at 250°F (120°C) for 1 hour.
4. Top with whipped cream and raspberries.

Scorpio's Dark Chocolate Chili Cake

Ingredients:

- 1 cup flour
- ½ cup cocoa powder
- ½ tsp cayenne pepper
- ½ tsp cinnamon
- 1 cup sugar
- ½ cup butter, melted
- 2 eggs

Instructions:

1. Mix flour, cocoa, cayenne, and cinnamon.
2. Beat sugar, butter, and eggs together, then combine with dry ingredients.
3. Bake at 350°F (175°C) for 30 minutes.

Sagittarius' Exotic Thai Green Curry

Ingredients:

- 1 lb chicken breast, sliced
- 2 tbsp green curry paste
- 1 can (14 oz) coconut milk
- 1 cup mixed vegetables (bell peppers, zucchini, eggplant)
- 2 tbsp fish sauce
- 1 tbsp brown sugar
- ½ cup fresh basil leaves
- 1 tbsp lime juice

Instructions:

1. Sauté curry paste in a pan until fragrant.
2. Add chicken and cook until browned.
3. Pour in coconut milk, fish sauce, and sugar.
4. Add vegetables and simmer for 10 minutes.
5. Stir in basil and lime juice, then serve.

Capricorn's Sophisticated Truffle Gnocchi

Ingredients:

- 1 lb potato gnocchi
- 2 tbsp butter
- 1 tbsp truffle oil
- ½ cup heavy cream
- ½ cup Parmesan cheese
- Salt and pepper to taste
- Fresh parsley for garnish

Instructions:

1. Cook gnocchi according to package instructions.
2. Melt butter in a pan, then add cooked gnocchi.
3. Stir in cream, Parmesan, and truffle oil.
4. Season and garnish with parsley before serving.

Aquarius' Inventive Miso Caramel Ice Cream

Ingredients:

- 2 cups heavy cream
- 1 cup whole milk
- ¾ cup sugar
- 3 tbsp white miso paste
- ½ cup caramel sauce

Instructions:

1. Heat milk, cream, and sugar until warm.
2. Whisk in miso paste and let cool.
3. Churn in an ice cream maker.
4. Swirl in caramel before freezing.

Pisces' Ethereal Blue Butterfly Pea Tea

Ingredients:

- 2 cups hot water
- 1 tbsp dried butterfly pea flowers
- 1 tbsp honey
- ½ lemon, juiced

Instructions:

1. Steep butterfly pea flowers in hot water for 5 minutes.
2. Strain, stir in honey, and squeeze in lemon juice.
3. Watch the color change and serve.

Aries' Spicy Kimchi Fried Rice

Ingredients:

- 2 cups cooked rice
- ½ cup chopped kimchi
- 1 tbsp kimchi juice
- 1 tbsp gochujang (Korean chili paste)
- 1 tbsp soy sauce
- 1 egg
- 2 green onions, sliced

Instructions:

1. Sauté kimchi in a pan, then add rice.
2. Stir in kimchi juice, gochujang, and soy sauce.
3. Top with a fried egg and green onions.

Taurus' Luxurious Lobster Thermidor

Ingredients:

- 2 lobster tails, cooked and halved
- 2 tbsp butter
- 1 shallot, minced
- ½ cup heavy cream
- ¼ cup white wine
- ½ cup Gruyère cheese, shredded
- 1 tsp Dijon mustard

Instructions:

1. Sauté shallots in butter, then add wine and reduce.
2. Stir in cream, mustard, and cheese.
3. Spoon sauce over lobster halves and broil for 5 minutes.

Gemini's Contrasting Sweet & Spicy Tofu Stir-Fry

Ingredients:

- 1 block firm tofu, cubed
- 2 tbsp soy sauce
- 1 tbsp honey
- 1 tbsp chili sauce
- 1 red bell pepper, sliced
- 2 green onions, chopped
- 1 tbsp sesame seeds

Instructions:

1. Sauté tofu until golden, then set aside.
2. Stir-fry bell pepper, then add tofu back.
3. Toss with soy sauce, honey, and chili sauce.
4. Garnish with green onions and sesame seeds.

Cancer's Cozy Clam Chowder in a Bread Bowl

Ingredients:

- 2 cups chopped clams
- 2 cups clam juice
- 1 cup heavy cream
- 2 potatoes, diced
- 1 onion, chopped
- 2 tbsp butter
- 2 bread bowls

Instructions:

1. Sauté onions in butter, then add potatoes and clam juice.
2. Simmer until potatoes are tender.
3. Stir in clams and cream, then serve in bread bowls.

Leo's Majestic Gold-Dusted Crème Brûlée

Ingredients:

- 2 cups heavy cream
- 4 egg yolks
- ½ cup sugar
- 1 tsp vanilla extract
- Gold dust for garnish

Instructions:

1. Heat cream and vanilla, then slowly whisk into egg yolks and sugar.
2. Pour into ramekins and bake in a water bath at 325°F (165°C) for 30 minutes.
3. Cool, then caramelize sugar on top with a torch.
4. Dust with gold before serving.

Virgo's Wholesome Grain Buddha Bowl

Ingredients:

- 1 cup quinoa, cooked
- ½ cup roasted chickpeas
- ½ cup steamed broccoli
- ½ avocado, sliced
- 2 tbsp tahini dressing
- 1 tbsp sunflower seeds

Instructions:

1. Assemble quinoa, chickpeas, broccoli, and avocado in a bowl.
2. Drizzle with tahini dressing and sprinkle with sunflower seeds.

Libra's Aesthetically Pleasing Charcuterie Board

Ingredients:

- Assorted cheeses (brie, cheddar, goat cheese, blue cheese)
- Cured meats (prosciutto, salami, chorizo)
- Fresh fruits (grapes, figs, apple slices)
- Nuts (almonds, walnuts)
- Crackers or baguette slices
- Honey and jam

Instructions:

1. Arrange cheeses, meats, fruits, and nuts in an artful, balanced manner on a large platter.
2. Add small bowls of honey and jam for dipping.
3. Serve with crackers or baguette slices.

Scorpio's Seductive Dark Cherry Reduction Steak

Ingredients:

- 2 steaks (ribeye or filet mignon)
- 1 cup dark cherries, pitted
- 1 tbsp balsamic vinegar
- 1 tbsp butter
- ½ cup red wine
- Salt and pepper to taste

Instructions:

1. Season steaks with salt and pepper, then sear in a hot pan with butter to desired doneness.
2. In the same pan, add cherries, vinegar, and red wine.
3. Let sauce reduce until thickened, then pour over steaks before serving.

Sagittarius' Global Street Food Sampler

Ingredients:

- 1 batch chicken satay with peanut sauce
- 1 batch crispy spring rolls
- 1 batch Mexican street corn (Elote)
- 1 batch Greek lamb skewers
- Dips: tzatziki, guacamole, sriracha mayo

Instructions:

1. Prepare each street food dish according to its recipe.
2. Arrange all items on a platter with various dips for a fun, multicultural spread.
3. Serve with skewers and small plates for easy sharing.

Capricorn's Well-Crafted Classic French Onion Soup

Ingredients:

- 2 large onions, thinly sliced
- 4 cups beef broth
- 1 cup white wine
- 1 baguette, sliced
- 1 ½ cups Gruyère cheese, grated
- 2 tbsp butter
- Salt and pepper to taste

Instructions:

1. Sauté onions in butter until golden and caramelized.
2. Add wine and cook until reduced, then pour in beef broth.
3. Simmer for 30 minutes and season to taste.
4. Serve in bowls, top with baguette slices and cheese, then broil until bubbly.

Aquarius' Unique Purple Sweet Potato Gnocchi

Ingredients:

- 2 cups mashed purple sweet potatoes
- 1 ½ cups flour
- 1 egg
- ½ tsp salt
- 2 tbsp olive oil

Instructions:

1. Mix mashed potatoes, flour, egg, and salt to form a dough.
2. Roll dough into logs, cut into pieces, and boil until they float.
3. Sauté gnocchi in olive oil until golden and crispy.

Pisces' Ocean-Inspired Blueberry Glazed Salmon

Ingredients:

- 2 salmon fillets
- 1 cup fresh blueberries
- 2 tbsp honey
- 1 tbsp balsamic vinegar
- 1 tsp Dijon mustard
- Salt and pepper to taste

Instructions:

1. Season salmon with salt and pepper, then pan-sear until cooked through.
2. In a small saucepan, combine blueberries, honey, vinegar, and mustard.
3. Simmer until sauce thickens, then spoon over salmon before serving.

Aries' Bold Sriracha-Lime Chicken Skewers

Ingredients:

- 1 lb chicken breast, cut into cubes
- 2 tbsp sriracha
- 1 tbsp lime juice
- 2 tbsp olive oil
- 1 tbsp soy sauce
- 1 tbsp honey

Instructions:

1. Combine sriracha, lime juice, olive oil, soy sauce, and honey in a bowl.
2. Marinate chicken cubes for at least 30 minutes.
3. Skewer chicken and grill until cooked through.

Taurus' Indulgent Slow-Cooked Short Ribs

Ingredients:

- 4 beef short ribs
- 2 cups beef broth
- 1 cup red wine
- 1 onion, chopped
- 3 garlic cloves, minced
- 2 tbsp tomato paste
- Salt and pepper to taste

Instructions:

1. Sear short ribs in a hot pan until browned on all sides.
2. Add onions, garlic, and tomato paste, cooking until softened.
3. Pour in wine and broth, then cover and slow-cook for 3-4 hours until tender.
4. Serve with a drizzle of sauce.

www.ingramcontent.com/pod-product-compliance
Lightning Source LLC
LaVergne TN
LVHW081507060526
838201LV00056BA/2988